My Best Book of Ballet

Angela Wilkes

KINGFISHER

Contents

Author and editor: Angela Wilkes
Consultants: Oonagh Phelan, Gwenda
  Grayson
Series editor: Camilla Reid
Designer: John Jamieson
Production manager: Oonagh Phelan
Illustrators: Terry Gabbey, Pamela
Goodchild, Christian Hook, Biz Hull, Nicki
Palin, Shirley Tourret, Andrew Wheatcroft
Photograph: Costume design on
page 23 is by Ian Spurling for *Elite
Syncopations* (1977)
DTP coordinator: Nicky Studdart

Every effort has been made to trace the
copyright holders of the photographs. The
Publishers apologise for any omissions.

KINGFISHER
Kingfisher Publications Plc,
New Penderel House,
283–288 High Holborn,
London WC1V 7HZ
www.kingfisherpub.com

First published in hardback by
Kingfisher Publications Plc 2000
10 9 8 7 6 5 4 3 2

2TR/0500/WKT/MAR(MAR)/128/KMA

First published in paperback by
Kingfisher Publications Plc 2002
10 9 8 7 6 5 4

4TR/0104/WKT/MAR(MAR)/130ENSOMA
1TS/0804/WKT/MAR(MAR)/128MA/F

A CIP catalogue record for this book
is available from the British Library.

ISBN 0 7534 0443 5 (hardback)
ISBN 0 7534 0672 1 (paperback)

Printed in China

Going to the ballet

When the lights dim and the curtain rises at the ballet, you enter another world. As the music swells up from the orchestra, dancers in colourful costumes leap and spin across the stage, acting out a story and creating graceful patterns of movement. Spellbound by the magical setting, you completely forget your surroundings.

In the spotlight

Moving spotlights shine down on the two principal dancers, forming small pools of light around them as they dance. Upstage, a group of dancers moves together, all doing the same steps as each other. These dancers are called the corps de ballet.

What is ballet?

 **Ballet is like a language, but it uses music and dance to tell a story instead of words.**

There are many different styles of ballet. Some of them are based on steps and techniques that have been passed down by dancers for over 300 years.

The Firebird

Les Sylphides

The Sleeping Beauty

Courtly dance

Ballet started in the 16th and 17th centuries in Italy and France. The dancer Maria Camargo shortened her skirt to show her clever footwork.

Romantic ballet

In the 1830s, many ballets created a supernatural world of spirits and ghosts. Ballerinas began to dance on pointe for the first time.

Classical ballet

Late 19th-century ballets tell dramatic stories. They are full of spectacular steps and lifts which require great skill and strength.

New expression

In the early 20th century, a Russian ballet company, the Ballets Russes, created a new, expressive style of ballet. Their ballets were danced to modern music and had bold costumes and stage sets.

The Firebird

Voluntaries

Folk dances

Classical ballets often include short national dances. These are based on folk dances from countries all around the world.

Modern ballet

Modern ballets borrow movements from many different styles of dance. Some of them are based on classical ballet steps interpreted in new ways.

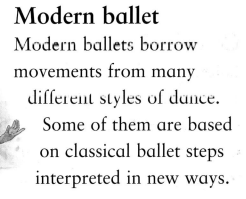

7

Famous ballets

Most of the famous
ballets follow the magical
adventures of princesses,
heroes, fairies and wizards.
Other ballets do not tell a story
but simply create a mood
or are even just
about dancing.

Giselle

Giselle, a village girl, dies
of a broken heart and
becomes a spirit. She saves
her lover from being killed
by the spirits of other girls.

The Nutcracker

Clara is given a nutcracker doll at a Christmas Eve party. As night falls, the doll turns into a soldier prince, and takes Clara on a magical journey to the Kingdom of Sweets.

The Sleeping Beauty

A wicked fairy casts a spell on a princess so she will die. A good fairy changes the spell so the princess falls asleep instead. After one hundred years, a prince breaks the spell by waking the princess with a kiss.

Swan Lake

Prince Siegfried falls in love with Odette, a princess who has been turned into a white swan by a magician. Odile, the magician's daughter, dresses up as a black swan and tricks Siegfried into promising to marry her.

Learning to dance

Ballet dancers start classes when they are children. At a ballet class you learn the basic steps and positions, and how to move to music. The exercises are simple versions of those professional ballet dancers do every day.

These children are waiting at the barre

The teacher tells you what to do and corrects you

Arm exercises teach you how to move your arms and hands expressively

Ballet class

Classes usually begin with warm-up exercises at the barre, a rail on the wall.

Then you move to the centre of the room to do more exercises, and sequences of slow and fast steps.

The pianist is playing the music for the class

Ribbons must be tucked in neatly

11

What to wear

Before you start a ballet class, ask your teacher what you should wear. It is important to wear stretchy, comfortable clothes that are easy to move in. They must also fit closely so that your teacher can see all your movements clearly and spot any mistakes you make. Your hair should be pinned neatly or tied back.

It is best to tie long hair in a bun, or plait it and then pin it to the top of your head

Girls' practice clothes

The best thing to wear is a leotard with tights. Little girls sometimes wear socks instead of tights. Dancers often wear legwarmers or a crossover cardigan until they have warmed up. In rehearsals, they sometimes wear a practice tutu as well.

Ballet shoes

Ballet shoes must fit well. For classes, girls wear flat satin or leather shoes fastened with elastic or ribbons. Boys wear flat shoes fastened with elastic. Shoes for character dancing have small heels. Look after your shoes carefully by keeping them tucked inside each other between classes.

Flat satin shoe with ribbons

Leather shoe with elastic

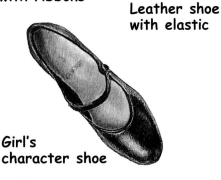

Girl's character shoe

Boys wear a T-shirt or leotard, shorts or tights, socks and flat leather or canvas shoes

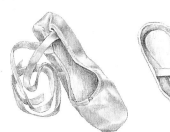

Tying your ribbons

1 Take the inside ribbon first and pass it across and around your ankle.

2 Pass the outside ribbon over and around your ankle, on top of the first one.

3 Tie the ribbons into a knot on the inside of your ankle and tuck in the ends.

13

Basic positions

In ballet there are five basic positions for the feet and arms. All ballet movements start and end with one of these positions, and dancers use them to move from one step to another. Dancers stand very straight, with their feet and legs turned out from the hips.

Head straight, with chin and eyes level

Arms should be softly rounded, as if you are holding a giant Easter egg

Legs should be turned out from the hips

First position

Stand with your heels together and your legs and feet turned out. Hold your hands slightly apart.

Keep your toes flat and the weight over the centre of your feet

Second position

Stand with your feet about shoulder-width apart. Hold your arms out to the sides in a smooth curve.

14

Hands and feet

Hold your hands with your fingers grouped together lightly and your thumbs tucked in.

Ballet dancers point their toes to make their legs look longer and more graceful. Point your feet in a straight line and try not to clench your toes.

First pliés

Pliés are knee bends. Dancers do them to stretch and warm up their muscles. You will start with small pliés in first position.

Third position
Cross one foot halfway in front of the other. Hold one arm curved in front and the other one out to the side.

Fourth position
Put one foot a little way in front of the other. Hold one arm above your head and the other out to the side.

Fifth position
Stand with the heel of your front foot against the toes of your back foot. Hold your arms above your head.

15

Step by step

After warming up at the barre, dancers go to the centre of the studio to practise other exercises.

They start with the slower steps, then move on to quick turns and jumps. Most ballet steps have French names because they were first set down in France.

On pointe

Dancing on pointe looks easy, but it is actually very hard. You can only start it after several years of training, when your feet and legs are strong enough. It is also very important to wear special pointe shoes.

Grand jeté

At the end of class, dancers practise big jumps across the studio. This jump is a grand jeté, which means big leap. The dancer stretches both legs out, like doing the splits in mid-air, and keeps his or her toes pointed.

In an attitude,
the lifted
leg makes a
rounded shape

Grand allegro

This jump is often
called a fish step
because the dancer
curves his body
like a fish.

Pirouette

A pirouette is a
spin or turn done
on one straight
leg with the other
leg tucked up.

Attitude

Here, the dancer
stands on one leg,
with the other leg
bent behind or in
front of her.

Arabesque

In this graceful position,
a dancer stands on one leg
and stretches the
other one
straight out
behind her.

**The man holds
the woman firmly
round her waist**

Lifts

To do difficult lifts
like this, the man has
to be strong and his
partner needs a good
sense of balance.

Acting a part

Ballet dancers have to be able to act as well as dance. Instead of words, they use body language, facial expression and mime to tell a story or express their feelings. All these things help to create a magical, exciting performance.

Petrushka cowers in fear

Mime

Mime uses a series of special gestures each of which has its own meaning. Dancers learn these gestures just as they learn their steps.

Giselle holds her head to show she feels as if she is going mad

Expressing feelings

Dancers show feelings by making all their movements larger than life. This helps the audience to understand what is happening.

'Death!'

'Why?'

'Please!'

18

Body language

Dancers use their whole bodies to tell you about a character. This dancer is stretching her neck like a swan and moving her arms to look like strong wings.

From class to stage

Ballet dancers train for many years. When girls join a ballet company they start in the corps de ballet. Later they may become soloists. The most talented go on to become principals.

1 All dancers start the day with a class, whether they are new to the company or a principal. This gives them a chance to work on their basic techniques.

2 Before class starts, dancers do simple stretching exercises to warm up. This helps to prevent injuries such as strained muscles.

3 Class starts with exercises at the barre. The steps are more difficult versions of the ones you do at a children's ballet class.

4 Later, dancers rehearse for different ballets. Partners practice together if they are going to dance a pas de deux – a dance specially for two people.

5 Between rehearsals there are often costume fittings. The dressmaker checks that new costumes fit well, look good and are comfortable to dance in.

6 Before a performance, dancers do their hair and make-up. Finally, they change into their costumes.

7 Most dancers feel nervous before a performance, but that helps them dance even better once on stage. The music takes over and they really enjoy dancing before an audience.

Creating a ballet

New ballets are created by people called choreographers. They choose the music and theme for the ballet and plan the steps. Then they work with dancers to try out their ideas. This helps them to decide on the movements for the ballet.

Music and notation

Choreographers sometimes ask a composer to write new music for a ballet. A person called a notator keeps a record of the steps for the ballet, by writing them down as symbols.

Musical score

Dance notation

Costume design

The costume designer does sketches of all the costumes for a new ballet. She or he also decides which fabrics and trimmings to use for each costume.

Stage set

The set designer plans the stage layout. He or she makes a model of it, complete with props, so the company director and choreographer can see what it will look like and check how it will work.

Behind the scenes

While dancers rehearse a new ballet, there is a huge team of people working backstage.

Some are preparing the scenery and lights, others are making costumes. Everything has to be ready in time for the first night.

Lighting

Lighting sets the mood for a ballet. Coloured lights, spotlights and special effects are all used to create atmosphere. The lights are set in place before each performance.

Costumes

The costumes for each ballet are made by the wardrobe department. They are made by machine, but all the trimmings and fastenings have to be sewn on by hand.

Painting scenery

The backcloths for the stage are often painted flat on the floor. A team of painters works from a grid showing them what to paint.

Rehearsing

This rehearsal for a modern ballet is taking place on stage, so that the dancers can find out exactly how much space they have. They are being coached by a former principal dancer.

Costume and make-up

Costume and make-up help dancers to create the characters they are playing and set the scene for the ballet. They can transform dancers into ghostly spirits, wicked wizards or even lifelike frogs!

Leotards

In modern ballets dancers often wear all-in-one leotards. These jazzy costumes from *Elite Syncopations* go with the ragtime music used in the ballet.

Ghostly spirits

In Romantic ballets, dancers wear white dresses, and sometimes wings. Their full skirts float as they move, to make them look like spirits.

Animal costumes

Realistic masks, like this frog mask from *The Tales of Beatrix Potter*, help the audience believe in the character. However, they can be very hot to dance in.

Classical tutu

The tutu is a short, stiff skirt made of layers of net. It leaves the dancer's legs free to perform jumps and lifts.

Basic stage make-up adds colour to the face and accentuates the eyes and mouth

Men also wear make-up, but it is less bright than women's

Make-up

All dancers do their own stage make-up. It exaggerates and brightens their features, so the audience can see their faces clearly under the strong stage lighting.

Dramatic character make-up alters the look of a dancer's face

Curtain up

At last, it is the first night – the curtain rises and the ballet begins. As some dancers perform, others wait their turn at the sides of the stage. Before ballerinas go on stage, they rub their shoes in rosin, to stop them slipping when they dance.

Backstage

The stage manager runs the show from her desk at the side of the stage. She calls the dancers to the stage, and tells the stagehands when to change the scenery and lights.

Curtain call

The ballet ends and thunderous applause breaks out as the curtain falls.
Then it rises again so that the whole company can take their bow. The soloists and finally the principals take their curtain calls. The performance is over.

The end of the day

After the performance, dancers usually eat. Then they go home to soak in a hot bath to ease their tired muscles. Tomorrow it will be time to start all over again!

Glossary

arabesque Position on one leg, with the other leg lifted and stretched behind the dancer to create a flowing line from fingertips to toes.

attitude Position on one leg, with the raised leg bent to form a curve either behind or in front of the dancer.

backcloth A painted cloth that hangs down at the back of the stage as part of the scenery.

barre The handrail on the wall that dancers use to help them balance when doing exercises.

character rôle Part in a ballet that requires more acting and mime than actual dancing.

choreographer Person who creates a ballet by arranging the steps and movements to music.

Classical ballet Ballet technique used particularly in late 19th-century ballets. These ballets are known as Classical ballets.

composer A person who writes music, including ballet music.

corps de ballet (cor de ballay) Dancers who perform together as a group and do not dance solos.

grand allegro (grond alaygroh) Big jumps and quick movements. Grand is the French word for big. Allegro is an Italian word meaning quick and lively.

grand jeté (gron jettay) Big leap with both legs stretched out, like doing the splits in mid-air.

leotard Stretchy costume, like a swimsuit with or without sleeves, that dancers wear for ballet classes and rehearsals.

mime A silent form of acting which uses movements and gestures to show feelings or tell a story, rather than words.

notator A person who records all the movements in a ballet, using a system of symbols called notation.

pas de deux (pa de duh) A dance for two people.

pirouette A fast turn on one straight leg, with the other bent. Pirouette means 'spinning top'.

plié (pleeay) This is the French word for 'bent'. Pliés are knee-bending exercises that dancers do when they are warming up.

pointe shoes Shoes with specially hardened toes that ballerinas wear so they can dance on the tips of their toes.

principal One of the leading dancers in a ballet company.

rôle The part that a dancer plays in a ballet.

Romantic ballet A style of ballet from the early 19th century, often featuring spirits.

rosin A powder made from tree resin, which dancers rub onto their shoes to stop them from slipping on the stage.

soloist A dancer who dances parts on their own, but not usually leading rôles.

tutu A ballerina's short, stiff skirt made of many layers of gathered net.

Index